TERMINOLOGY of MANAGEMENT AND FINANCIAL ACCOUNTANCY

THE INSTITUTE OF COST AND MANAGEMENT ACCOUNTANTS
63 PORTLAND PLACE LONDON WIN 4AB

First published 1974
Reprinted (with minor revisions) 1977
Reprinted 1978
Reprinted (with minor revisions) 1980

ISBN 0 901308 30 7

Institute of Cost & Management Accountants
Secretary: T B Degenhardt MA FCIS
Registered Offices & Library
63 Portland Place
London W1N 4AB
Telephone: 01-637 4716
Telegrams: ICAMA London W1N 4AB

FOREWORD

This terminology, issued with the authority of the Council of the Institute, is the third major revision of the original Costing Terminology since this was first published in March 1937, in the Institute's Journal.

The revised edition contains working definitions of terms in management accounting (including cost accounting) and also in financial accounting, thus providing the accountant with definitions of the 'tools of his trade.'

In framing the definitions, note has been taken of the views expressed by a wide range of experienced assessors. Where it became apparent that differing points of view would need to be recognised, appropriate comment has been introduced, stating an alternative usage or indicating a preference.

The publication of this terminology should not restrict the development of new and informative forms of expression which may in the future prove to be more useful than those now in use. For the present, however, it is believed that this terminology, like its predecessors, will be widely adopted.

DENYS EDMONDS
President

1974.

'I am not yet so lost in lexicography, as to forget that words are the daughters of earth, and that things are the sons of heaven.'

Dictionary of the English Language
Dr. Samuel Johnson

INTRODUCTION

The diversity of the activities which concern the accountant in his duties is such that no universally applicable set of terms and definitions can ever be devised. Those set out in this book are offered with the hope that they will be appropriate to the majority of situations.

The terms have been classified and assembled in accordance with their context, so that related terms will be found together. Individual terms should be traced through the Index, which covers both parts of the book; Part 1 dealing with management accounting and Part 2 with financial accounting. It will be seen that in certain cases (e.g. net profit) a term which carries one meaning in management accounting may have a different meaning when used in the financial accounts.

For ease of reference each term has been allotted a numerical symbol, unique to that term. It will be realized that the number of digits in a symbol arises from the position of the term to which it relates in the contextual structure, and is in no way a measure of the importance of the term in relation to others.

Accountancy continues to evolve to meet changing needs. The terms selected for inclusion, and their definitions, are intended to reflect the evolutionary stage now reached, and outmoded terms have been omitted.

Regard has been paid to legislation, and to the Statements of Standard Accounting Practice, in currrent force.

For simplicity the term 'business' has been used as a general term to embrace all types of organization, except where the context demands otherwise (as in the treatment of the term 'company').

The needs of the student have been borne in mind throughout, Those taking the Institute's examinations, in particular. should make themselves familiar with the book.

Acknowledgements.

The Institute's gratitude is due in particular to Mr. E. Laidler, F.C.M.A., assisted by Mr. A. H. Fleet, F.C.M.A., for his pioneering work in developing the coordinated concept of variance accounting, suggesting many of the definitions and for his later work in producing the final text.

Thanks are due also to the many people who have helped in the preparation of this terminology and particularly to those members of the Institute's major Committees on Education and Training, Examinations, Post Qualifying Education and Research and Technical matters, who acted as assessors to Mr. J. R. S. Wagener, C.A., and to the Technical Advisory Department, Peat, Marwick Mitchell & Co., who were kindly made available as advisers on Part 2.

Note on Variance Accounting

It will be seen that standard costing, budgetary control and variance analysis have been dealt with in the context of the overall concept of variance accounting.

The term 'standard costing' originated some sixty years ago, when it was appropriate to the original concept to which it referred. However, evolution has broadened the concept to the point that variance statements now usually commence with the operating profit variance, the analysis of which then proceeds, stage by stage, through all sections of the revenue and cost structure.

The term 'budgetary control' is also of long standing. Historically, the two terms, budgetary control and standard costing, appear to have referred to two distinct techniques although, by reason of the complementary role of each to the other, it was inevitable that, by process of evolution, they would eventually merge into a single concept.

Where standard product costs are prepared, and where charging rates for overhead are required, these are derived from the budget, whereas the amounts to be included in the budget in respect of prime costs are based on the standard costs. The budget and the standard costs both play their part in the process of variance analysis, and a management accountant preparing a statement of variances would regard as quite pointless any attempt to define where budgetary control ended and standard costing began, or to classify the variances into two separate theoretical sectors. His objective is the single one of accounting for all variances which have affected the operating profit. The technique is therefore a triunity involving budgets, standard costs and the process of variance analysis.

Neither of the terms budgetary control nor standard costing is wide enough to cover the unified technique, and the combined term, 'budgetary control and standard costing' is both unwieldy and illogical, as it brings together two incompatible terms. Taken literally, one refers to a control technique and the other to a costing method, but it is widely accepted that both budgets and standard costs are used for purposes of control, and that both are concerned with costs. The accountant applying the unified technique is accounting for variances, and so it is felt that the introduction of the term **variance accounting** is justified.

In those situations where budgets are in use but standard costs are not, either of the terms budgetary control or variance accounting would be appropriate.

Note to 1977 Reprint:

The following definitions have been revised since first publication:

8.254
8.331
8.332

Note to 1980 Reprint:

The following definitions have been revised or added:

1.1	8.246.1
3.221.4	8.336.4
3.221.5	8.336.5
3.242	9.103
3.34	9.104
8.106	9.105
8.106.1	9.25
8.217	

CONTENTS

SCHEDULE OF DIAGRAMS

PART 1

MANAGEMENT ACCOUNTANCY

Table 1

The table below shows the broad divisions into which the terms in this part of the Terminology have been classified.

1. FUNCTIONS	1.1 Management accounting 1.2 Cost accounting 1.3 Costing 1.4 Cost audit
2. THE SYSTEM	2.1 Link with financial accounts 2.2 Basic costing methods 2.3 Superimposed principles and techniques 2.4 Cost allotment procedures 2.5 Accounting periods
3. VALUES	3.1 Selling price 3.2 Cost 3.3 Profit 3.4 Variances 3.5 Control ratios
4. RECORDS	4.1 Documents 4.2 Ledgers 4.3 Accounts 4.4 Budgets 4.5 Standing instructions

MANAGEMENT ACCOUNTANCY

Table 2

The table which follows gives a complete contextual classification of the terms in this part of the Terminology.

Note: * Denotes a heading only – the term is not defined.

1. **Functions***
    - 1.1 Management accounting
    - 1.2 Cost accounting
    - 1.3 Costing
    - 1.4 Cost audit

2. **The system***
    - 2.1 Link with financial accounts*
        - 2.11 Interlocking accounts
        - 2.12 Integral accounts
    - 2.2 Basic costing method
        - 2.21 Specific order costing
            - 2.211 Job costing
            - 2.212 Batch costing
            - 2.213 Contract costing
        - 2.22 Operation costing
            - 2.221 Process costing
            - 2.222 Service costing
    - 2.3 Superimposed principles and techniques
        - 2.301 Absorption costing
        - 2.302 Marginal costing
        - 2.311 Actual cost ascertainment
        - 2.312 Variance accounting
            - 2.312.1 Standard costing
            - 2.312.2 Budgetary control
            - 2.312.3 Variance analysis
        - 2.313 Differential costing
        - 2.314 Incremental costing
        - 2.315 Uniform costing

2.4 Cost allotment procedures*
- 2.41 Cost allocation
- 2.42 Cost apportionment
- 2.43 Overhead absorption
  - 2.431 Direct wages percentage rate
  - 2.432 Direct labour hour rate
  - 2.433 Machine hour rate
  - 2.434 Cost unit rate
  - 2.435 Standard cost rate
- 2.44 Valuation of stores issues*
  - 2.441 First in, first out price (FIFO)
  - 2.442 Last in, first out price (LIFO)
  - 2.443 Replacement price
  - 2.444 Weighted average price
  - 2.445 Standard price

2.5 Accounting period*
- 2.51 Costing period
- 2.52 Budget period
- 2.53 Control period

3. **Values***

3.1 Selling price*
- 3.11 Standard selling price
- 3.12 Retention money
- 3.13 Transfer price

3.2 Cost
- 3.21 Elements of cost
  - 3.211 Materials cost
  - 3.212 Wages cost
  - 3.213 Expenses
  - 3.214 Prime cost
    - 3.214.1 Direct materials cost
    - 3.214.2 Direct wages cost
    - 3.214.3 Direct expenses
  - 3.215 Overhead
    - 3.215.1 Indirect materials cost
    - 3.215.2 Indirect wages cost
    - 3.215.3 Indirect expenses

Note: * Denotes a heading only – the term is not defined

3.215.4 Absorbed overhead
3.215.5 Over-absorbed overhead
3.215.6 Under-absorbed overhead

3.22 Objective costs*

(This category includes items which, though not strictly costs, either enter into the calculations of costs, or are things or activities the costs of which are ascertained.)

- 3.221 Costs of major functions*
  - 3.221.1 Production cost
  - 3.221.2 Marketing cost
    - 3.221.21 Selling cost
    - 3.221.22 Publicity cost
    - 3.221.23 Distribution cost
  - 3.221.3 General administration cost
  - 3.221.4 Research cost
  - 3.221.5 Development cost
- 3.222 Cost centre
  - 3.222.1 Process cost centre
  - 3.222.2 Production cost centre
  - 3.222.3 Service cost centre
- 3.223 Budget centre
- 3.224 Profit centre
- 3.225 Costs of products*
  - 3.225.01 Cost unit
  - 3.225.02 Job
  - 3.225.03 Batch
  - 3.225.04 Contract
  - 3.225.05 Equivalent units
  - 3.225.06 Net realizable value
  - 3.225.07 By-product
  - 3.225.08 Joint products
  - 3.225.09 Waste
  - 3.225.10 Scrap
  - 3.225.11 Spoilage
  - 3.225.12 Production cost of sales
  - 3.225.13 Total cost of sales
  - 3.225.14 Conversion cost
  - 3.225.15 Added value

Note: * Denotes a heading only – the term is not defined

- 3.23 Fixed and variable costs*
  - 3.231 Period cost
  - 3.232 Fixed cost
  - 3.233 Variable cost
    - 3.233.1 Variable production overhead
    - 3.233.2 Variable production cost
    - 3.233.2 Variable marketing cost
  - 3.234 Semi-variable cost
  - 3.235 Marginal cost
  - 3.236 Budget control basis
  - 3.237 Budget cost allowance
- 3.24 Standard cost
  - 3.241 Standard performance
  - 3.242 Standard hour
  - 3.243 Basic standard
  - 3.244 Current standard
  - 3.245 Expected standard
  - 3.246 Normal standard
  - 3.247 Ideal standard
- 3.25 Miscellaneous costs*
  - 2.251 Controllable (or managed) cost
  - 3.252 Non-controllable cost
  - 3.253 Notional cost
  - 3.254 Opportunity cost

3.3 Profit
- 3.31 Contribution
- 3.32 Operating profit
- 3.33 Net profit
- 3.34 Attributable profit (on contracts)

The following terms (from 3.4 to 3.47) relate to the **operating profit variance** and its component parts. See diagram 3.

3.4 Operating profit variance
- 3.41 Operating profit variance due to sales
  - 3.411 Operating profit variance due to selling prices
  - 3.412 Operating profit variance due to sales volume
- 3.42 General administration cost variance
- 3.43 Marketing cost variance

Note: * Denotes a heading only – the term is not defined.

3.431 Fixed marketing cost variance
4.432 Variable marketing cost variance
3.44 Production cost variance
3.441 Fixed production overhead variance
3.441.1 Fixed production overhead expenditure variance
3.441.2 Fixed production overhead volume variance
3.441.21 Capacity variance
3.441.22 Fixed cost productivity variance
3.442 Variable production cost variance
3.442.1 Direct materials cost variance
3.442.11 Direct materials price variance
3.442.12 Direct materials usage variance
3.442.121 Direct materials mix variance
3.442.122 Direct materials yield variance
3.442.2 Direct wages cost variance
3.442.21 Direct wages rate variance
3.442.22 Direct labour efficiency variance
3.442.3 Variable production overhead variance
3.45 Budget revision variance (not shown on diagram 3)
3.46 Stock valuation revision variance (not shown on diagram 3)
3.47 Method variance (not shown on diagram 3)

3.5 Control ratios*
3.51 Ratios concerning production *(See diagram 4)
3.511 Production volume ratio
3.511.1 Capacity ratio
3.511.2 Productivity (or efficiency) ratio
3.52 Ratios concerning profitability
3.521 Return on capital employed ratio
3.521.1 Profit to sales ratio
3.521.2 Sales to capital employed ratio
3.522 Contribution to sales ratio
3.523 Margin of safety

4. Records*

4.1 Documents
4.11 Basic documents
4.111 Goods received note
4.112 Materials requisition
4.113 Materials returned note

Note: * Denotes a heading only – the term is not defined.

4.114 Materials transfer note
4.115 Labour transfer note
4.116 Employee's time record
4.117 Machine time record
4.118 Cost journal voucher
4.12 Intermediate documents*
4.121 Materials cost analysis sheet
4.122 Wages analysis sheet
4.123 Expenses analysis sheet
4.124 Overhead distribution sheet
4.125 Inventory
4.13 Cost sheets, statements, charts, etc.*
4.131 Cost estimate sheet/card
4.132 Cost sheet/card/statement
4.133 Standard cost sheet/card
4.134 Operating statement
4.135 Break-even chart

4.2 Ledgers*
4.21 Cost Ledger
4.22 Subsidiary ledger
4.23 Stores ledger
4.24 Work in progress ledger
4.25 Finished goods stock ledger
4.26 Overhead ledger

4.3 Accounts*
4.31 Cost account
4.32 Control account
4.33 Contra account
4.34 Cost ledger contra account
4.35 Clearing account
4.36 Suspense account

4.4 Budgets
4.41 Master budget
4.42 Functional budget
4.43 Basic and current budgets*
4.431 Basic budget
4.432 Current budget

Note: * Denotes a heading only – the term is not defined.

Note: * Denotes a heading only — the term is not defined

MANAGEMENT ACCOUNTANCY

The profession whose members practise management accounting, and the complex of principles, techniques and methods by means of which their expertise is put into effect.

1. FUNCTIONS

1.1 Management accounting
The preparation and presentation of accounting information in such a way as to assist management in the formulation of policies and in the planning and control of the activities of the undertaking.

1.2 Cost accounting
The application of accounting and costing principles, methods and techniques in the ascertainment of costs and the analysis of savings and/or excesses as compared with previous experience or with standards.

1.3 Costing
The ascertainment of costs.

1.4 Cost audit
The verification of cost records and accounts and a check on the adherence to the prescribed cost accounting procedures and the continuing relevance of such procedures.

2. THE SYSTEM

2.1 Link with Financial Accounts

2.11 Interlocking accounts
A system in which the cost accounts are distinct from the financial accounts, the two sets of accounts being kept continuously in agreement or readily reconcilable.

Note: With the possible exception of certain special items of income and expenditure which are purposely treated in one set of accounts only, the same basic data are used in both sets of accounts.

2.12 Integral accounts
A single set of accounts which provides both financial and management accounting information.

DIAGRAM 1

MANAGEMENT ACCOUNTING
METHODS, PRINCIPLES AND TECHNIQUES
related to the routine system

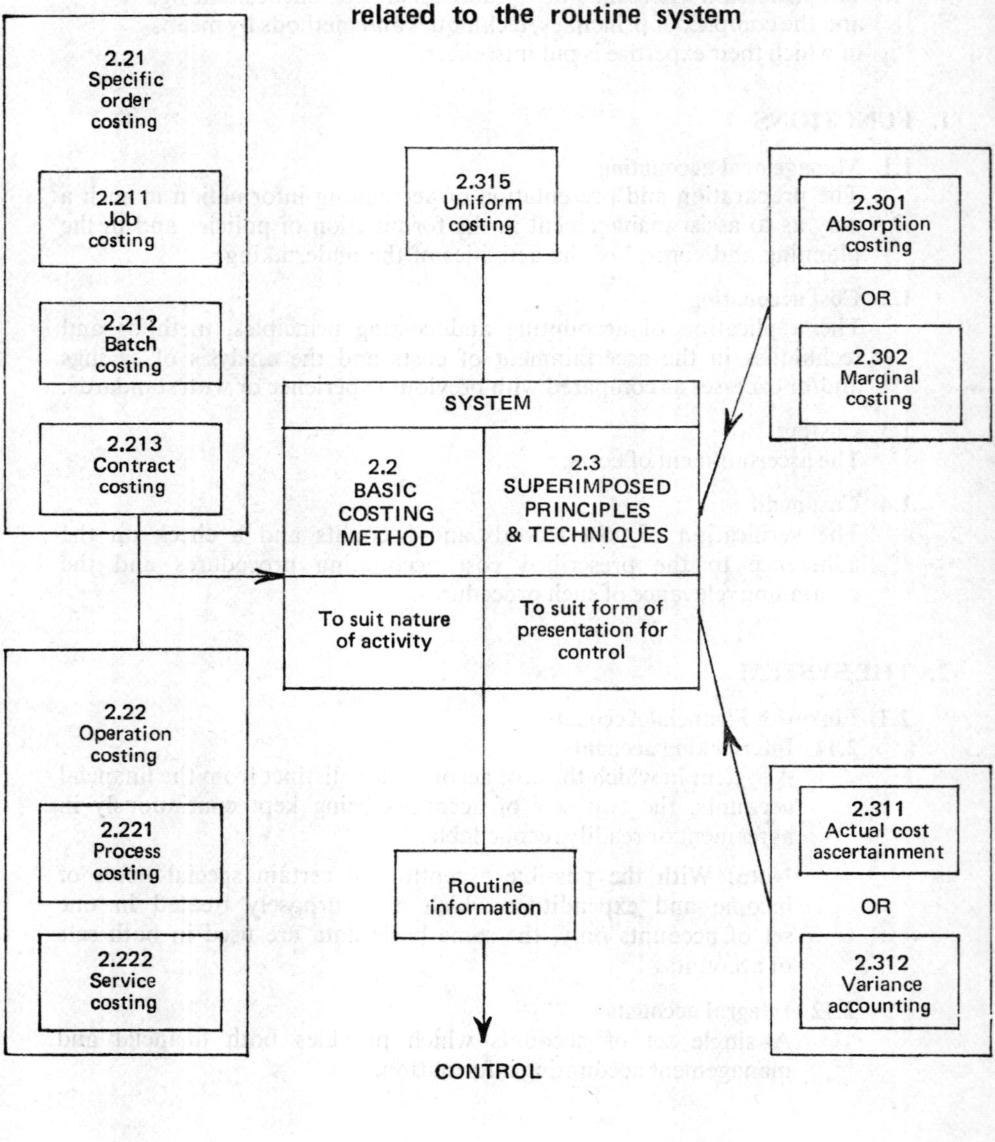

2.2 Basic costing method

A method of costing which is devised to suit the methods by which goods are manufactured or services are provided. (See diagram 1).

2.21 Specific order costing

The category of basic costing methods applicable where the work consists of separate contracts, jobs or batches, each of which is authorized by a special order or contract. (See diagram 1).

2.211 Job costing

That form of specific order costing which applies where work is undertaken to customers' special requirements. As distinct from contract costing, each job is of comparatively short duration. The work is usually carried out within a factory or workshop where each job moves through the processes or operations as a continuously identifiable unit, although the term may also be applied to such work as property repairs carried out on the customer's premises. (See diagram 1).

Note: The method may also be used in the costing of internal capital expenditure jobs.

2.212 Batch costing

That form of specific order costing which applies where similar articles are manufactured in batches either for sale or for use within the undertaking. In most cases the costing is similar to job costing. (See diagram 1).

2.213 Contract costing

That form of specific order costing which applies where work is undertaken to customers' special requirements and each order is of long duration (compared with those to which job costing applies). The work is usually of a constructional nature. In general the method is similar to job costing, although it has certain distinctive features. (See diagram 1).

2.22 Operation costing

The category of basic costing methods applicable where standardized goods or services result from a sequence of repetitive and more or less continuous operations or processes to which costs are charged before being averaged over the units produced during the period. (See diagram 1).

2.221 Process costing

That form of operation costing (see 2.22) which applies where standardized goods are produced. (See diagram 1).

2.222 Service costing

That form of operation costing (see 2.22) which applies where standardized services are provided either by an undertaking or by a service cost centre within an undertaking. The method may be used where the service is not completely standardized but where it is convenient to regard it as such, and to calculate average costs per period in relation to the standardized unit or measurement, e.g. ton-mile in the case of goods transport or patient-day in the case of hospitals. (See diagram 1).

2.3 Superimposed principles and techniques

Principles and techniques devised to suit the manner in which it is decided to present information to management. (See diagram 1).

2.301 Absorption costing

A principle whereby fixed as well as variable costs are allotted to cost units. The term may be applied where (a) production costs only, or (b) costs of all functions are so allotted. (See diagram 1).

2.302 Marginal costing

A principle whereby marginal costs of cost units are ascertained. Only variable costs are charged to cost units, the fixed costs attributable to a relevant period being written off in full against the contribution for that period. (See diagram 1).

Note: It is recommended that the term be applied only where the *routine* system incorporates the marginal principle. (See 2.313 differential costing).

2.311 Actual cost ascertainment

A principle whereby costs of cost centres and cost units are ascertained which, subject to certain approximations, are deemed to represent actual costs. (The term 'historical costing' is often used to describe this concept but is not recommended because the word 'historical' may equally be applied to other concepts, e.g. statements of variances related to past events). (See diagram 1).

2.312 Variance accounting

A technique whereby the planned activities of an undertaking are expressed in budgets, standard costs, standard selling prices and standard profit margins, and the differences between these and the comparable actual results are accounted for. Management is periodically presented with an analysis of differences by causes and responsibility centres, such analysis usually commencing with the operating profit variance. The technique also includes the establishment of a suitable arrangement of accounts in the principal ledger. (See diagram 1).

2.312.1 Standard costing

The preparation of standard costs of products and services. See Standard cost (3.24) and Variance accounting (2.312).

2.312.2 Budgetary control

The establishment of budgets relating the responsibilities of executives to the requirements of a policy, and the continuous comparison of actual with budgeted results, either to secure by individual action the objective of that policy or to provide a basis for its revision.

Note: The term **variance accounting** is more appropriate where planned performances are expressed in standard costs per unit of product or service as well as in budgets, all being used in comparisons with actual results.

2.312.3 Variance analysis

That part of variance accounting (2.312) which relates to the analysis into constituent parts of variances between planned and actual performance. (See diagram 3 and definitions 3.4—3.47).

2.313 Differential costing

A technique used in the preparation of ad hoc information in which only cost and income differences between alternative courses of action are taken into consideration.

2.314 Incremental costing

A technique used in the preparation of ad hoc information where consideration is given to a range of graduated changes in the level or nature of activity. The additional costs and revenues likely to result from each degree of change are presented.

2.315 Uniform costing

The use by several undertakings of the same costing systems, i.e. the same basic costing methods and super-imposed principles and techniques.

2.4 Cost allotment procedures

2.41 Cost allocation

The allotment of whole items of cost to cost centres or cost units. (See also 2.42.)

2.42 Cost apportionment

The allotment to two or more cost centres of proportions of common items of cost on the estimated basis of benefit received. (See also 2.41.)

2.43 Overhead absorption

The allotment of overhead to cost units by means of rates separately calculated for each cost centre. In most cases the rates are predetermined.

2.431 Direct wages percentage rate

A rate calculated by dividing the estimated overhead cost attributable to a cost centre by the amount of direct wages expected to be incurred, or which would relate to working at normal capacity, and expressing the result as a percentage.

2.432 Direct labour hour rate

A rate calculated by dividing the estimated overhead cost attributable to a cost centre by the appropriate number of direct labour hours. This may be either the number of hours expected to be worked, or the number of hours which would relate to working at normal capacity.

2.433 Machine hour rate

A rate calculated by dividing the estimated overhead cost attributable to a machine or group of similar machines by the appropriate number of machine hours. This may be either the number of hours for which the machine or group is expected to be operated, or the number of hours which would relate to working at normal capacity.

2.434 Cost unit rate

A rate calculated by dividing the estimated overhead cost attributable to a cost centre by either the number of cost units expected to be produced in that cost centre, or by the number related to working at normal capacity.

2.435 Standard cost rate

A rate calculated by dividing the expected overhead cost attributable to a cost centre by the predetermined quantity of the base to which the rate is applied.

2.44 Valuation of stores issues

2.441 First In, First Out Price (FIFO)

The price paid for the material first taken into the stock from which the material to be priced could have been drawn

2.442 Last In, First Out Price (LIFO)

The price paid for the material last taken into the stock from which the material to be priced could have been drawn.

2.443 Replacement price

The price at which material could be purchased, identical to that which is being replaced or revalued.

2.444 Weighted average price

A price which is calculated by dividing the total cost of materials in the stock from which the material to be priced could be drawn, by the total quantity of materials in that stock.

2.445 Standard price

A predetermined price fixed on the basis of a specification of all factors affecting that price.

DIAGRAM 2

THE ELEMENTS OF COST
related to a typical manufacturing organization

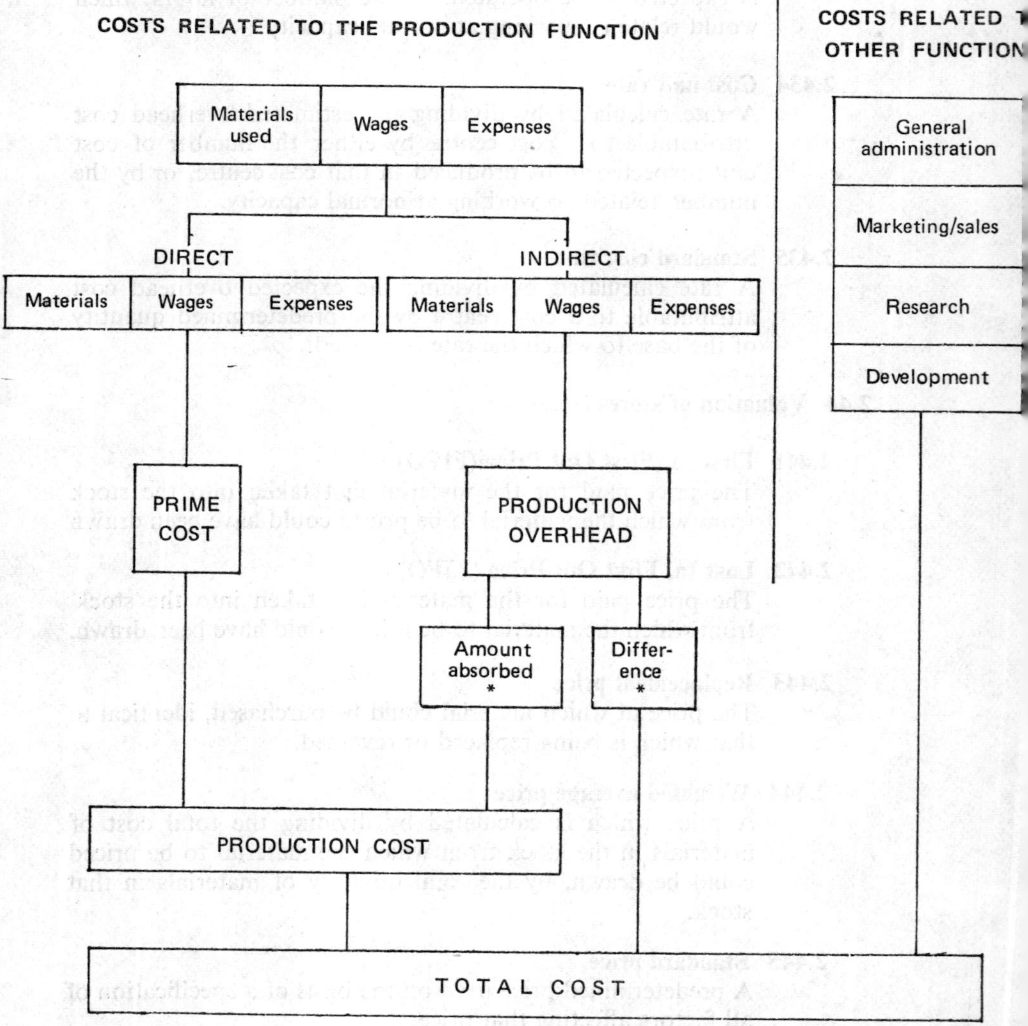

* Note: In the case of marginal costing, the amount of production overhead absorbed would relate to the variable category only

2.5 Accounting period

2.51 Costing period

A period in respect of which costs are ascertained. A typical costing period would be four or five weeks or a calendar month.

2.52 Budget period

The period for which a budget is prepared and used.

2.53 Control period

A period in respect of which comparisons are made between budgeted and actual results. It is usually the same as the costing period. (See 2.51).

3. VALUES

3.1 Selling price

3.11 Standard selling price

A predetermined selling price which may be used in connection with variance accounting. (See 2.312).

3.12 Retention money

A sum of money representing an agreed proportion of a price for goods supplied or work completed, such proportion being withheld by the purchaser or contractee for an agreed period of time as security against failure by the supplier or contractor to fulfil his obligations under the terms of the contract.

3.13 Transfer price

A price related to goods or other benefits transferred from one process or department to another or from one member of a group to another. The extent to which costs and profit are covered by the price is a matter of policy.

3.2 Cost

1. (as a noun). The amount of expenditure (actual or notional) incurred on, or attributable to, a specified thing or activity. (See diagram 2).
2. (as a verb). To ascertain the cost of a specified thing or activity.

Note: the word 'cost' can rarely stand alone and should be qualified as to its nature and limitations.

3.21 Elements of cost

The primary classification of costs according to the factors upon which expenditure is incurred, vizl., materials, wages and expenses. (See diagram 2).

3.211 Materials cost

The cost of commodities, other than fixed assets, introduced into products or consumed in the operation of an organisation. (See diagram 2).

3.212 Wages cost

The cost of employees' remuneration. (See diagram 2).

Note: for the specific purposes of individual enterprises the term would require more precise definition. Some may prefer to classify salaries of managers and clerical staff as wages, whilst others may not. Some may prefer to treat holiday pay and employers' contributions towards national insurance and pension fund as wages whilst others may not.

3.213 Expenses

All costs other than materials and wages. (See diagram 2).

3.214 Prime cost

The total cost of direct materials, wages and expenses. The term prime cost is commonly restricted to direct production costs only and so does not customarily include direct costs of marketing or research and development. (See diagram 2 and definitions 3.214.1/3).

3.214.1 Direct materials cost

The cost of materials entering into and becoming constituent elements of a product or saleable service. (See diagram 2, also 3.211, materials cost).

3.214.2 Direct wages cost

The cost of remuneration for employees' efforts and skills applied directly to a product or saleable service. (See diagram 2).

3.214.3 Direct expenses

Costs, other than materials or wages, which are incurred for a specific product or saleable service. (See diagram 2).

3.215 Overhead

The total cost of indirect materials, wages and expenses. (See diagram 2).

Note: the synonymous term **burden** is in common use in the U.S.A. and in subsidiaries of American companies in the U.K.

3.215.1 Indirect materials cost

Materials cost other than direct materials cost.

3.215.2 Indirect wages cost

Wages cost other than direct wages cost.

3.215.3 Indirect expenses

Expenses, other than direct expenses.

3.215.4 Absorbed overhead

Overhead which, by means of absorption rates, is included in costs of specific products or saleable services.

3.215.5 Over-absorbed overhead

The amount by which overhead absorbed exceeds the amount of overhead incurred.

3.215.6 Under-absorbed overhead

The amount by which overhead incurred exceeds the overhead absorbed.

3.22 Objective costs

3.221 Costs of major functions

3.221.1 Production cost

Prime cost (3.214) plus absorbed production overhead. (See diagram 2).

3.221.2 Marketing cost

The cost incurred in publicizing and presenting to customers the products of the undertaking in suitably attractive forms and at acceptable prices, together with the costs of all relevant research work, the securing of orders and, usually, delivery of the goods to customers. (See diagram 2 and 3.221.23, distribution cost). In certain cases, after-sales service and/or order processing may also be included.

3.221.21 Selling cost

That portion of marketing cost which is incurred in securing orders.

3.221.22 Publicity cost

That portion of marketing cost which is incurred in advertising and promotion as aids to the eventual sales of goods or services.

3.221.23 Distribution cost

That portion of marketing cost which is incurred in warehousing saleable products and in delivering products to customers.

Note: in most cases, particularly where consumer products are concerned, distribution is regarded as a part of the marketing function but, in exceptional cases – for example, where heavy industrial equipment is supplied – distribution may be regarded as an extension of the production function.

3.221.3 General administration cost

The sum of those costs of general management, and of secretarial, accounting and administrative services, which cannot be directly related to the production, marketing, research or development functions of the enterprise. (See diagram 2).

3.221.4 Research cost

The cost of original investigation undertaken in order:

(a) to gain new scientific or technical knowledge and understanding. Basic research is not primarily directed towards any specific practical aim or application.

(b) to gain new scientific or technical knowledge and directed towards a specific practical aim or objective.
(*Definition from SSAP 13*).

3.221.5 Development cost
The cost of using scientific or technical knowledge in order to produce new or substantially improved materials, devices, products, processes, systems or services prior to the commencement of commercial production.
(*Definition from SSAP 13*).

3.222 Cost centre
A location, person or item of equipment (or group of these) in respect of which costs may be ascertained and related to cost units. (See 3.225.01 cost unit).

3.222.1 Process cost centre
A cost centre in which a specific process or a continuous sequence of operations is carried out.

3.222.2 Production cost centre
A cost centre in which production is carried on.

3.222.3 Service cost centre
A cost centre for the provision of a service or services to other cost centres.

Note: this term does not usually apply when the output of an organization is a service, rather than goods.

3.223 Budget centre
A section of an organization defined for the purposes of budgetary control. (See 2.312.2, budgetary control).

3.224 Profit centre
A division of an organization to which both expenditure and revenue are attributable and in respect of which profitability can be assessed.

3.225 Costs of products

3.225.01 Cost unit
A quantitative unit of product or service in relation to which costs are ascertained.

3.225.02 Job (Defined in relation to costing method).
A cost unit which consists of a single specific order. (See 2.211, job costing).

3.225.03 Batch (Defined in relation to costing method).
A cost unit which consists of a group of similar articles which maintains its identity throughout one or more stages of production. (See 2.212, batch costing).

3.225.04 Contract (Defined in relation to costing method).
A cost unit which consists of a single contract. (See 2.213, contract costing).

3.225.05 Equivalent units
A notional quantity of completed units substituted for an actual quantity of incomplete physical units in progress, when the aggregate work content of the incomplete units is deemed to be equivalent to that of the substituted quantity (e.g. 150 units 50 per cent. complete=75 equivalent units). The principle applies when operation costs are being apportioned between work in progress and completed output.

Note: the synonymous term 'effective unit' is not recommended.

3.225.06 Net realizable value (Defined in relation to by-product).

The estimated selling price (net of trade discounts but before deducting settlement discounts), less all attributable costs incurred after separation from the main product. (See 3.225.07, by-product).

3.225.07 By-product

A product which is recovered incidentally from the material used in the manufacture of recognized main products, such by-product having either a net realizable value (see 3.225.06) or a usable value, such value being relatively unimportant in comparison with the saleable value of the main products. By-products are usually subjected to further processing after separation from the main product.

Note: whilst definitions of by-product, joint products, waste and scrap are offered in this Terminology, it is emphasised that a clear distinction between these terms is not always possible or even necessary. An item regarded as a by-product in one factory may be termed either a joint product or scrap in another. The use of common sense, with due regard to the circumstances in valuing the item and in treating it in the accounts, is more important than the term applied.

3.225.08 Joint products

Two or more products separated in the course of processing, each having a sufficiently high saleable value to merit recognition as a main product. (See Note under 3.225.07, by-product).

3.225.09 Waste

Discarded substances having no value. (See Note under 3.225.07, by-product).

3.225.10 Scrap

Discarded material, having some recovery value, which is usually either disposed of without further treatment (other than reclamation and handling), or re-introduced into the production process in place of raw material. (See Note under 3.225.07, by-product).

3.225.11 Spoilage

Units of output which fail to reach the required standard of quality or specification. Such faulty units may be capable of rectification, and may be so corrected if the cost of doing so is less than the loss in value from allowing the fault to remain uncorrected. When it is uneconomic to rectify a fault,

the article may be sold as sub-standard if it is still functionally sound; otherwise it may be disposed of as scrap.

3.225.12 Production cost of sales

The production cost of the products sold during a specified accounting period.

3.225.13 Total cost of sales

The total cost of production, marketing, general administration and research and development, attributable to the products or services sold during a specified accounting period.

3.225.14 Conversion cost

The sum of the production costs of converting purchased materials into finished products, i.e. direct wages, direct expenses and absorbed production overhead.

3.225.15 Added value

The increase in market value resulting from an alteration in the form, location or availability of a product or service, excluding the cost of bought-out materials or services.

Note: unlike conversion cost, added value includes profit.

3.23 Fixed and variable costs

3.231 Period cost. (See 3.232, fixed cost).

3.232 Fixed cost

A cost which accrues in relation to the passage of time and which, within certain output or turnover limits, tends to be unaffected by fluctuations in volume of output or turnover. Examples are rent, rates, insurance and executive salaries.

3.233 Variable cost

A cost which, in the aggregate, tends to vary in direct proportion to changes in the volume of output or turnover.

3.233.1 Variable production overhead

Overhead cost related to production which, in the aggregate, tends to vary in direct proportion to changes in the volume of output.

Note: factors other than the volume of physical output can influence the amount of variable production overhead, e.g. the number of persons employed, the number of direct labour hours worked or the number of machine hours. It is not, however, usually practicable to identify and measure these influences with sufficient precision to merit their acceptance as a basis for further analysing variable production overhead variance (3.442.3). (See diagram 3).

3.233.2 Variable production cost

The sum of prime cost (3.214) and variable production overhead (3.233.1).

3.233.3 Variable marketing cost

A cost related to marketing (3.221.2) which, in the aggregate, tends to vary in direct proportion to changes in the volume of turnover.

3.234 Semi-variable cost

A cost containing both fixed and variable elements, which is therefore partly affected by fluctuations in the volume of output or turnover.

3.235 Marginal cost
The variable cost of one unit of a product or a service; i.e. a cost which would be avoided if the unit was not produced or provided.

Note: in this context a unit is usually either a single article or a standard measure such as the gallon (or litre), pound weight (or kilogram) etc., but may in certain circumstances be an operation, process or part of an organization.

3.236 Budget control basis
The nature of a cost (that is, variable, semi-variable or fixed) which determines the manner in which the budget cost allowance (3.237) is calculated.

3.237 Budget cost allowance
The cost which a budget centre would be expected to incur in a control period (2.53), having regard to the budget control bases (3.236) which apply. This usually comprises variable costs in direct proportion to the volume of production or service achieved, and fixed costs as a proportion of the annual budget, having regard to the spread, throughout the year, of benefits expected to be der ved from the expenditure, rather than to the dates of payment. (**Standard allowance** is a synonymous term).

3.24 Standard cost
A predetermined cost calculated in relation to a prescribed set of working conditions, correlating technical specifications and scientific measurements of materials and labour to the prices and wage rates expected to apply during the period to which the standard cost is intended to relate, with an addition of an appropriate share of budgeted overhead. Its main purposes are to provide bases for control through variance accounting (2.312), for the valuation of stocks and work in progress, and, in exceptional cases, for fixing selling prices.

3.241 Standard performance
The rate of output which qualified workers can achieve without over-exertion as an average over the working day or shift provided they adhere to the specified method and

provided they are motivated to apply themselves to their work. (*Definition from BS 3138; 1979*).

3.242 Standard unit of work

A unit of work, expressed in terms of standard hours or standard minutes, consisting of the basic time for carrying out an element of work plus relexation allowance and contingency allowance where applicable. (*Definition based on BS 3138; 1979*).

3.243 Basic standard

An underlying standard from which a current standard (3.244) can be developed.

3.244 Current standard

A standard established for use over a short period of time, related to current conditions.

3.245 Expected standard

The standard which it is anticipated can be attained during a future specified budget period.

3.246 Normal standard

The average standard which it is anticipated can be attained over a future period of time, preferably long enough to cover one trade cycle.

3.247 Ideal standard

The standard which can be attained under the most favourable conditions possible.

3.25 Miscellaneous costs

3.251 Controllable *or* managed cost

Cost, chargeable to a budget or cost-centre, which can be influenced by the actions of the person in whom control of the centre is vested.

Note: it is not always possible to pre-determine responsibility, because the reason for deviation from expected performance may only become evident from subsequent investigation. For example, excessive scrap may arise from inadequate supervision or from some latent defect in purchased material.

3.252 Noncontrollable cost
A cost chargeable to a budget or cost centre which cannot be influenced by the actions of the person in whom control of the centre is vested (see note following definition of controllable cost: 3.251).

3.253 Notional cost
A hypothetical cost taken into account to represent a benefit enjoyed by the undertaking in respect of which no actual expense is incurred.

3.254 Opportunity cost
The value of a benefit sacrificed in favour of an alternative course of action.

3.3 Profit
The financial gain resulting from a transaction or combination of transactions, being the excess of sales revenue over related costs.

3.31 Contribution. **(1) Contribution per unit.** The difference between the selling price of a unit of product or service and its marginal cost (3.235). **(2) Contribution in total.** The difference between the sales value and the variable cost (3.233) of such sales.

3.32 Operating profit
The profit arising from the normal activities of the business, such as the provision and sale of manufactured goods or services, before taking account of extraneous transactions such as those of a purely financial nature.

3.33 Net profit
(1) The profit remaining after all further expenses and/or losses have been deducted from the operating profit (3.32) and further revenues have been added. (2) The profit of a business before distribution but after deducting from net sales all direct and

indirect costs incurred in making those sales. Net profit can be stated before or after taxation.

3.34 Attributable profit (on contracts)

That part of the total profit currently estimated to arise over the duration of the contract (after allowing for likely increases in costs so far as not recoverable under the terms of the contract) which fairly reflects the profit attributable to that part of the work performed at the accounting date. (There can be no attributable profit until the outcome of the contract can be assessed with reasonable certainty). (*Definition from SSAP 9*).

DIAGRAM 3

VARIANCE ANALYSIS

NOTES: (1) Where a numerical symbol is followed by letter 'A' or 'M', the letter indicates if the term relates to the absorption costing concept (A), or to the marginal costing concept (M). If neither letter follows the numerical symbol the term is common to both concepts.

(2) (*) The asterisked terms are abbreviated. For the full versions see the definitions.

(3) The analytical pattern shown below is theoretical and is intended to indicate general principles. It is emphasised that variance analysis, like all management accounting procedures, must be devised to suit the conditions prevailing within the particular enterprise.

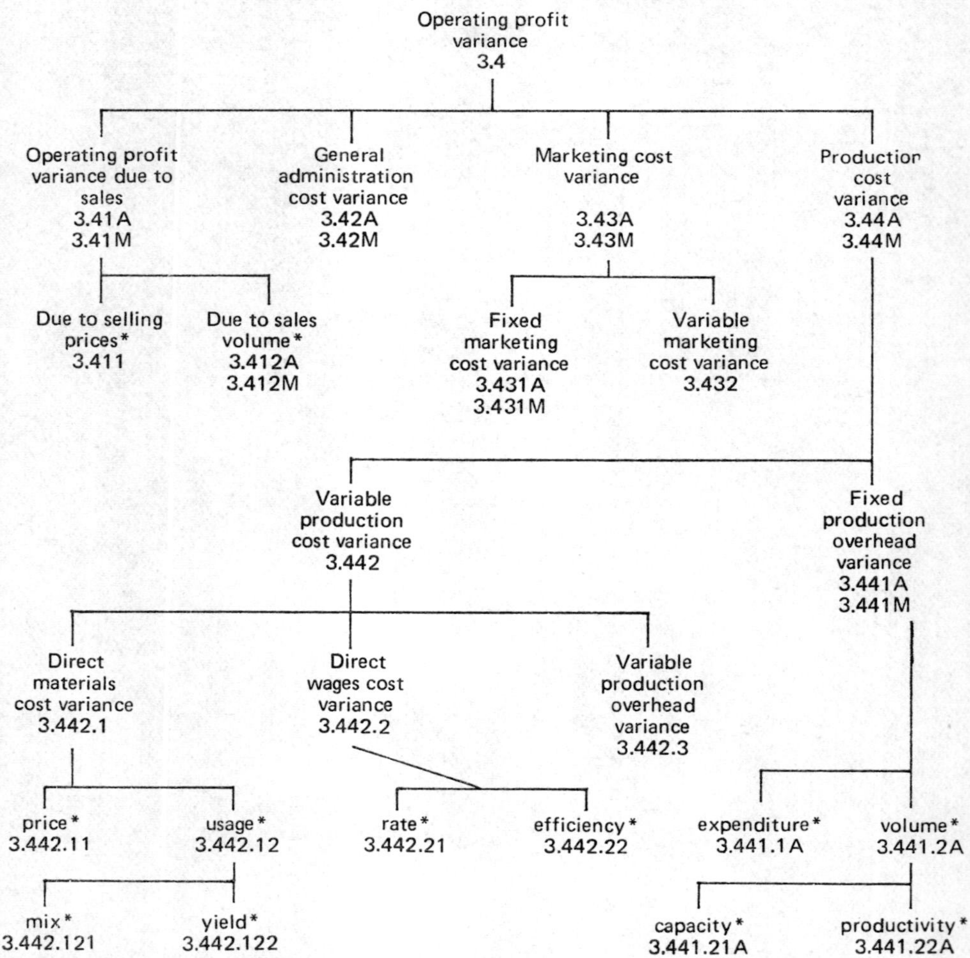

THE OPERATING PROFIT VARIANCE & ITS COMPONENT PARTS

The inter-relationships of the following variances, 3.4 to 3.442.3 inclusive, are illustrated by diagram 3.

Where a numerical symbol is followed by 'A' or 'M', the letter indicates whether the term relates to the absorption costing concept (A), or to the marginal costing concept (M). If neither letter follows the numerical symbol the definition is common to both concepts.

3.4 Operating profit variance
The difference between budgeted and actual operating profit related to a specific period. (See operating profit, 3.32).
Note: this variance would not be entered in a ledger account as budgeted operating profit does not appear therein.

Operating profit variance due to sales

3.41A The difference between (a) the budgeted operating profit and (b) the margin between the actual sales and the standard cost of those sales.

3.41M The difference between (a) the budgeted contribution and (b) the margin between the actual sales and the standard variable cost of those sales. (See contribution, 3.31).

Note: this variance, and those which are part of it, would not be entered in a ledger account, as budgeted profit does not appear therein.

3.411 Operating profit variance due to selling prices
The difference between the standard and actual prices of the sales effected.

Operating profit variance due to sales volume

3.412A The difference between budgeted and actual sales quantities, both being valued at standard unit operating profit margins.

3.412M The difference between budgeted and actual sales quantities, both being valued at standard unit contribution margins. (See contribution, 3.31).

General administration cost variance

3.42A The difference between the total standard cost of general administration included in the total standard cost of the products sold and the actual expenditure incurred on general administration. Such expenditure would usually be deemed to be fixed in nature. If it is considered worth while, this variance can be analysed into expenditure and sales volume variances.

3.42M The difference between the budget cost allowance (3.237) for general administration (3.221.3) for a specified control period (2.53) and the amount of actual expenditure attributed and charged to that period. This variance represents expenditure differences only.
(See footnote to 3.441.1A).

Marketing cost variance

3.43A The difference between the total standard cost of marketing (3.221.2) included in the total standard cost of the products sold and the actual expenditure incurred on marketing.

3.43M The sum of fixed and variable marketing cost variances (3.431M and 3.432).

Fixed marketing cost variance

3.431A The difference between the standard cost of fixed marketing overhead absorbed in the cost of sales achieved, and the fixed marketing overhead attributed and charged to the period. If it is considered worth while, this variance can be analysed into expenditure and sales volume variances.

3.431M The difference between the budget cost allowance (3.237) for marketing for a specified control period (2.53) and the amount of actual fixed expenditure attributed and charged to that period. This variance represents expenditure differences only.
(See footnote to 3.441.1A).

3.432 Variable marketing cost variance

The difference between the standard and actual variable marketing costs of the products actually sold.

See also diagram 3, page 30

Production cost variance

3.44A The difference between the standard cost of production achieved during the period, whether completed or not (see footnote), and the actual cost incurred on such work (see 3.221.1, productions cost).

Note: the most typical form of industrial activity features a series of operations, with quantities of unfinished work remaining in operation at the end of each costing period. Consequently, it is usually pointless to attempt to relate total costs of materials used and work done during a period to the completed output of the same period.

3.44M The sum of the fixed production overhead variance (3.441M) and the variable production cost variance (3.442).

Fixed production overhead variance

3.441A The difference between the standard cost of fixed overhead absorbed in the production achieved, whether completed or not, and the fixed overhead attributed and charged to that period. (See footnotes to 3.44A and 3.441.1A).

3.441M The difference between the budget cost allowance (3.237) for production for a specified control period (2.53) and the amount of actual fixed expenditure attributed and charged to that period. This variance represents expenditure differences only and so corresponds with 3.441A, the footnote to which should be referred to.

3.441.1A Fixed production overhead expenditure variance

The difference between the budget cost allowance (3.237) for production for a specified control period (2.53) and the amount of actual fixed expenditure attributed and charged to that period.

Note: as many items of fixed overhead occur annually, or in relation to other periods of time which do not coincide with control periods, the amounts attributed and charged to particular periods, as with the budget cost allowances, are based on accountancy decisions which take into account the spread throughout the year of benefits derived from the expenditure rather than the dates of payment.

See also diagram 3, page 30

3.441.2A Fixed production overhead volume variance
That portion of the fixed production overhead variance which is the difference between the standard cost absorbed in the production achieved, whether completed or not, and the budget cost allowance (3.237) for a specified control period (2.53).

3.441.21A Capacity variance
That portion of the fixed production overhead volume variance which is due to working at higher or lower capacity than standard. Capacity is often expressed in terms of average direct labour hours worked per day, and the variance is the difference between the budget cost allowance (3.237) and the actual direct labour hours worked (valued at the standard hourly absorption rate).

3.441.22A Fixed cost productivity variance
That portion of the fixed production overhead volume variance which is the difference between the standard cost absorbed in the production achieved, whether completed or not, and the actual direct labour hours worked (valued at the standard hourly absorption rate).

3.442 Variable production cost variance
The difference between the standard variable cost of the production achieved, whether completed or not, and the actual variable cost incurred on such work.
Note: the most typical form of industrial activity features a series of operations, with quantities of unfinished work remaining in operation at the end of each costing period. Consequently, it is usually pointless to relate total costs of materials used and work done during a period to the completed output of the same period.

3.442.1 Direct materials cost variance. (a) *when materials are charged to production at actual prices.* The difference between the standard cost of direct materials specified for the production achieved, whether completed or not, and the actual cost of direct materials used. (See footnote to 3.442). (b) *when materials are charged to production at standard prices.* The sum of the price and usage variances.
See also diagram 3, *page* 30

3.442.11 Direct materials price variance. (a) *when materials are charged to production at actual prices.* That portion of the direct materials cost variance which is the difference between the standard prices specified and the actual prices paid for the direct materials used. (b) *when materials are charged to production at standard prices.* That portion of the direct materials cost variance which is the difference between the standard price and the actual price paid for direct materials purchased during that period.

3.442.12 Direct materials usage variance

That portion of the direct materials cost variance which is the difference between the standard quantity specified for the production achieved, whether completed or not, and the actual quantity used, both valued at standard prices. (See footnote to 3.442).

3.442.121 Direct materials mix variance

That portion of the direct materials usage variance which is the difference between the actual quantities of ingredients used in a mixture at standard price, and the total quantity of ingredients used at the weighted average price per unit of ingredients as shown by the standard cost sheet (4.133).

(Applicable only when direct materials are physically mixed).

3.442.122 Direct materials yield variance

That portion of the direct materials usage variance which is the difference between the standard cost of the production achieved, whether completed or not, and the cost of that production, arrived at by multiplying the actual total quantity of ingredients used by the weighted average price per unit as shown by the standard cost sheet (4.133).

(Applicable only when direct materials are physically mixed).

See also diagram 3, page 30

3.442.2 Direct wages cost variance
The difference between the standard direct wages specified for the production achieved, whether completed or not, and the actual direct wages incurred. (See footnote to 3.442).

3.442.21 Direct wages rate variance
That portion of the direct wages cost variance which is the difference between the standard rates of pay specified and the actual rates paid.

3.442.22 Direct labour efficiency variance
That portion of the direct wages cost variance which is the difference between the standard direct wages cost for the production achieved, whether completed or not, and the actual hours at standard rates (plus incentive bonus, if any). (See footnote to 3.442).

3.442.3 Variable production overhead variance
The difference between the standard variable production overhead absorbed in the production achieved, whether completed or not, and the actual variable production overhead. (See footnote to 3.442).

Note: sub-division of this variance is not recommended unless there are reasonable grounds for believing that the resultant sub-variances would be sufficiently realistic to be helpful to management. (See also the note following the definition of variable production overhead, 3.233.1).

See also diagram 3, page 30

3.45 Budget revision variance

The difference between a basic and a revised standard cost, multiplied by the budgeted quantity for the period. It arises when an interim adjustment of a standard cost is made without adjusting the budget, and it is required in order that the difference between budgeted and actual profit may be fully analysed.

Note: this variance would not be entered in a ledger account as budgeted profit does not appear therein.

3.46 Stock valuation revision variance

The difference arising when stocks and work in progress which are valued at standard costs are revalued at new standard costs. This variance occurs particularly at the commencement of a new financial year.

3.47 Method variance

The difference between the standard cost of an operation performed by the standard method specified and the standard cost of the operation performed by the alternative method actually employed.

DIAGRAM 4

RATIOS CONCERNING PRODUCTION

These ratios may be calculated where quantities of goods produced or services provided can be expressed in terms of either standard direct labour hours or standard machine hours.

Each of the three ratios is related to a fixed overhead variance as shown in the diagram.

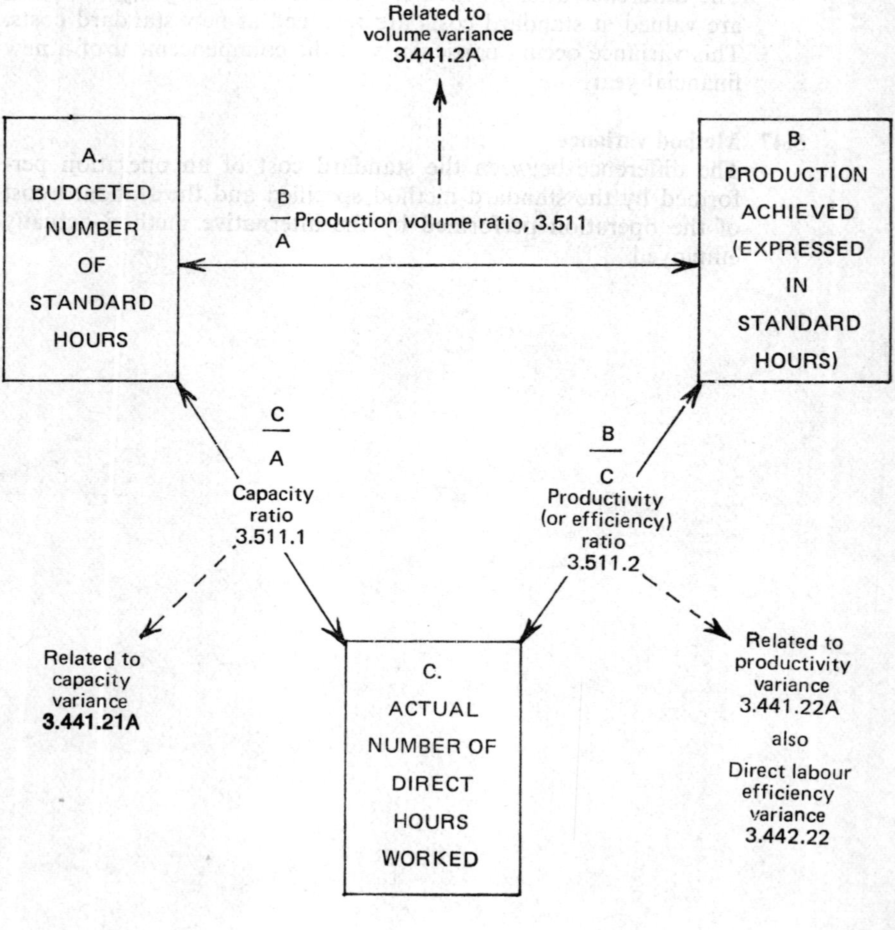

3.5 Control ratios

3.51 Ratios concerning production (see diagram 4)

3.511 Production volume ratio

The number of standard hours equivalent to the production achieved, whether completed or not, divided by (or expressed as a percentage of) the budgeted number of standard hours. (See diagram 4).

Notes: (i) this ratio is related to the fixed production overhead volume variance (3.441.2A).

(ii) the term 'activity ratio,' is synonymous but it is not recommended, as the word 'activity' is capable of different interpretations.

3.511.1 Capacity ratio

The actual number of direct working hours divided by (or expressed as a percentage of) the budgeted number of standard hours (see diagram 4).

Note: this ratio is related to the capacity variance (3.441.21A).

3.511.2 Productivity (*or* efficiency) ratio

The standard hours equivalent to the production achieved, whether completed or not, divided by (or expressed as a percentage of) the actual number of direct working hours. (See diagram 4).

Note: this ratio is related to the fixed cost productivity variance (3.441.22A) as well as to the direct labour efficiency variance (3.442.22).

3.52 Ratios concerning profitability

3.521 Return on capital employed ratio

The relationship between the profit earned (usually before tax) and the capital employed in earning that profit. It is normally expressed as a percentage, which measures the efficiency with which the capital is employed.

The term **primary ratio** is often used as an alternative.

3.521.1 Profit to sales ratio

The percentage which profit (before tax) bears to the value of sales.

3.521.2 Sales to capital employed ratio

The value of sales obtained for every £1 of capital employed.

3.522 Contribution to sales ratio

The relationship, usually expressed as a percentage, between contribution and sales value.

Note: the abbreviation 'P/V ratio' is not recommended.

3.523 Margin of safety

The excess of normal or actual sales over sales at break-even point (see 4.135, break-even chart). It may be expressed as a percentage of either normal or actual sales, whichever is selected for consideration.

4. RECORDS

4.1 Documents

4.11 Basic documents

4.111 Goods received note
A form recording all details relating to a receipt of materials from an outside source.

4.112 Materials requisition
A document which authorizes and records the issue of material for use.

4.113 Materials returned note
A document which records the return of unused material to store.

4.114 Materials transfer note
A document which records the transfer of material from one store to another, from one cost centre to another, or from one cost unit to another.

4.115 Labour transfer note
A document which records the transfer of labour from one cost centre to another, or from one cost unit to another.

4.116 Employee's time record
A document which records the amount of time spent by an employee and shows the analysis between a number of activities during a day or week. It may also show the wages relating to the recorded times.

4.117 Machine time record
A document which records the amount of time a machine is operated or remains idle. It may also record the cost of the time so recorded and details of the production achieved.

4.118 Cost journal voucher
A document which provides the details necessary to support an entry in the cost accounts.

4.12 Intermediate documents

4.121 Materials cost analysis sheet

A record showing the total materials cost (3.211) chargeable for a period and detailing the separate amounts relating to different cost units (3.225.01) or cost centres (3.222). The record is compiled mainly by summarizing material requisitions, material returned notes and material transfer notes. In certain cases there may be a separate section relating to specific purchases directly chargeable to cost units or cost centres where stores transactions do not arise.

4.122 Wages analysis sheet

A record showing the total amount of wages cost (3.212) incurred during a period and detailing the separate amounts relating to individual cost units (3.225.01) or cost centres (3.222).

4.123 Expenses analysis sheet

A record showing the total amount of expenses (3.213) chargeable for a costing period (2.51) and detailing the separate amounts relating to individual cost units (3.225.01) and cost centres (3.222).

4.124 Overhead distribution sheet

A columnar form used for the purpose of distribution of overhead expenditure over cost centres, and for the apportionment of the accumulated expenses of service cost centres over others.

4.125 Inventory

A list of quantities and values of stocks and work in progress.

4.13 Cost sheets, statements, charts, etc.

4.131 Cost estimate sheet/card

A document which provides for the assembly of the estimated detailed cost in respect of a cost centre or cost unit.

4.132 Cost sheet/card/statement

A document which provides for the assembly of the detailed cost of a cost centre or cost unit. (The term **job sheet** or **job card** may be preferred where the cost unit is a specific job).

4.133 Standard cost sheet/card

A document which provides for the assembly of the detailed standard cost of a unit or batch of product. The selling price and the contribution or profit may also be shown.

4.134 Operating statement

A summary of the operating costs (and where appropriate, of the income and profit margins) of the whole or part of the activities of an undertaking for a specified period.

Note: where variance accounting is applied, operating statements will usually provide information regarding the units produced in the period, the comparison of actual and standard or budgeted costs, income and profit margins, and an analysis of the variances.

4.135 Break-even chart

A chart which indicates approximate profit or loss at different levels of sales volume within a limited range. The level at which neither profit nor loss is shown is termed the break-even point.

4.2 Ledgers

4.21 Cost ledger

The principal ledger in the cost accounting book-keeping system where this is distinct from but interlocked with the financial accounts. It contains, inter alia, a number of control accounts which control subsidiary ledgers, and a contra account by means of which the double entry principle is maintained.

4.22 Subsidiary ledger

A supporting ledger consisting of a group of accounts of a similar nature the total of which is in agreement with a control account in the principal ledger. Its main purposes are to limit the accounts in the principal ledger to a manageable number, to simplify the location of errors by making each group self-balancing and to facilitate the delegation of clerical responsibilities. Examples are subsidiary ledgers maintained for creditors, stores, work in progress and finished stocks.

4.23 Stores ledger

A subsidiary ledger containing an account for each separately identifiable class of material handled by the stores organization. It is controlled by the stores control account in the principal ledger. It is sometimes referred to as the **raw materials ledger.**

4.24 Work in progress ledger

A subsidiary ledger containing detailed accounts of work in progress. It is controlled by the work in progress control account in the principal ledger. The work in progress accounts may take the form of printed cards or sheets on which costs are computed.

4.25 Finished goods stock ledger

A subsidiary ledger containing an account for each separately identifiable class of saleable product. It is controlled by the finished goods stock control account in the principal ledger.

4.26 Overhead ledger

A subsidiary ledger containing detailed accounts of overhead. It is controlled by the overhead control account in the principal ledger. The accounts in this ledger are arranged analytically, having regard to the main functions of the business, to the cost centres and to the different types of overhead cost.

4.3 Accounts

4.31 Cost account

An account in the cost ledger.

4.32 Control account

An account in the principal ledger (i.e. general ledger or cost ledger) having the purpose of controlling a subsidiary ledger. The transactions which are recorded in detail in individual accounts within the subsidiary ledger are entered in summary form in the control account. The balance of the account should always equal the total of the balances on the individual accounts in the subsidiary ledger.

4.33 Contra account

An account contained within a ledger for the purpose of maintaining the double entry principle.

4.34 Cost ledger contra account

A contra account (4.33) contained within the cost ledger (4.21). The term cost ledger *control* account is not recommended, as a cost ledger contra account does not control a subsidiary ledger. Its purpose is not, as is sometimes suggested, to effect agreement with the financial accounts (there are more effective ways of doing this) but to maintain the double entry principle.

4.35 Clearing account

An account which provides a convenient means of collecting different entries forming part of a whole amount which can then be transferred to other accounts, e.g. wages, where net wages, PAYE tax, national insurance, etc., must be aggregated before the gross wages can be analysed into direct and indirect.

Note: the term 'control account' is not recommended in such cases.

4.36 Suspense account

A ledger account in which items are held temporarily until sufficient information is available for them to be posted to the correct accounts.

4.4 Budgets

Financial and/or quantitative statements, prepared and approved prior to a defined period of time, of the policy to be pursued during that period for the purpose of attaining a given objective. They may include income, expenditure and the employment of capital.

For satisfactory control, budgets require regular review and modification to reflect rapidly changing conditions in the business environment, e.g. a business may operate **continuous budgeting** on a quarterly cycle.

4.41 Master budget

A budget which is prepared from, and summarizes, the functional budgets (see 4.42 below). The term **summary budget** is synonymous.

4.42 Functional budget

A budget of income or expenditure appropriate to, or the responsibility of, a particular function.

4.43 Basic and current budgets

4.431 Basic budget

A budget based on a long term plan and used as a basis for developing current budgets. A basic budget is usually much broader in scope and less detailed than a current budget.

4.432 Current budget

A budget which is established for use over a short period of time, usually one year but sometimes less, and related to current conditions. Current conditions may be interpreted as the average conditions likely to prevail during the budget period.

4.44 Fixed and flexible budgets

4.441 Fixed budget

A budget which is designed to remain unchanged irrespective of the volume of output or turnover attained.

4.442 Flexible budget

A budget which, by recognizing the difference in behaviour between fixed and variable costs in relation to fluctuations in output or turnover, is designed to change appropriately with such fluctuations.

4.45 Forecast

A prediction of future events in the light of circumstances expected to prevail. It differs from a budget in that it does not take account of special action which may be taken by management to alter the course of events.

4.46 Limiting factor

The factor which, at a particular time, or over a period, will limit the activities of an undertaking. The limiting factor is usually the level of demand for the products or services of the undertaking but it could be a shortage of one of the productive resources, e.g. skilled labour, raw material, or machine capacity, In order to ensure that the functional budgets are reasonably capable of fulfilment, the extent of the influence of this factor must first be assessed. (Also known as **key factor** or **principal budget factor**).

4.5 Standing instructions

4.51 Cost manual

A document which sets out standing instructions, governing the responsibilities of persons, and the procedures, forms and records relating to the costing system.

4.52 Budget manual

A document which sets out standing instructions governing the responsibilities of persons, and the procedures, forms and records relating to the preparation and use of budgets.

4.53 Classification

The arrangement of items in a logical sequence having regard to their nature (**subjective classification**) or the purpose to be fulfilled (**objective classification**).

4.54 Code

A system of symbols designed to be applied to a classified set of items.

In costing systems, **composite symbols** are commonly used. For example, in the composite symbol 211.392 the first three digits might indicate the nature of the expenditure (**subjective classification**) whilst the last three digits might indicate the cost centre or cost unit to be charged (**objective classification**).

PART 2

FINANCIAL ACCOUNTANCY

Table 1

The table below shows the broad divisions into which the terms in this part of the Terminology have been classified.

6. FUNCTIONS	6.1 Financial accounting 6.2 Bookkeeping 6.3 Financial audit
7. BOOKS AND RECORDS	7.1 Basic concepts 7.3 Ledgers and accounts 7.2 Books of prime entry
8. FINANCIAL STATEMENTS	8.1 Basic concepts 8.2 The balance sheet 8.3 Revenue reporting
9. NATURE & CONDITION OF ORGANIZATION	9.1 Nature 9.2 Condition

FINANCIAL ACCOUNTANCY

TABLE 2

The table which follows gives a complete contextual classification of the terms in this part of the Terminology.

Note: * Denotes a heading only – the term is not defined.

6 Functions*

6.1 Financial accounting
6.2 Book-keeping
6.3 Financial audit

7 Books and Records*

7.1 Basic concepts

7.101 Account
7.102 Posting
7.103 Debit entry
7.104 Credit entry
7.105 Contra
7.106 Double entry book-keeping
7.107 Single entry book-keeping
7.108 Balance (on an account)
7.109 Trial balance
7.110 Books of account
7.111 Cut-off date

7.2 Books of prime entry*

7.201 Day book
7.202 Journal
7.203 Purchases day book
7.204 Purchases returns book *or* returns outwards book
7.205 Sales day book
7.206 Sales returns book *or* returns inwards book
7.207 Cash book
7.207.1 Bank reconciliation
7.208 Petty cash book
7.208.1 Imprest

7.3 Ledgers and accounts*

7.301 General, impersonal *or* nominal ledger
7.302 Purchase *or* bought ledger
7.303 Sales ledger
7.304 Personal account
7.305 Real *or* property account
7.306 Nominal account
7.307 Impersonal account
7.308 Suspense account
7.309 Current account
7.310 Open account
7.311 Control account

8. Financial statements

8.1 Basic concepts*

8.101 Fundamental accounting concepts
8.102 Accounting bases
8.103 Accounting policies
8.104 Annual accounts
8.105 Accounting period
8.106 Group *and* Consolidated accounts
8.107 Cash flow

8.2 Balance sheet

8.21 Share capital and reserves*

8.211 Share (in a joint stock company)
- 8.211.1 Ordinary shares
- 8.211.2 Preference shares
  - 8.211.21 Cumulative preference shares
  - 8.211.22 Participating preference shares
  - 8.211.23 Redeemable preference shares
- 8.211.3 Deferred *or* founders' shares
- 8.211.4 Minority interests
- 8.211.5 Bonus *or* scrip issue
- 8.211.6 Rights issue
- 8.211.7 Non-voting shares
- 8.211.8 Nominee holding

Note: * Denotes a heading only – the term is not defined.

8.212 Share capital*
  8.212.1 Authorised, nominal *or* registered
  8.212.2 Issued *or* subscribed
  8.212.3 Unissued
  8.212.4 Called-up
  8.212.5 Uncalled
  8.212.6 Paid-up
  8.212.7 Equity share capital
  8.212.8 Prior charge capital
8.213 Reserves
  8.213.1 Capital reserves
  8.213.2 Revenue reserves
8.214 Share premium
  8.214.1 Share premium account
8.215 Equity
8.216 Net worth
8.217 Equity method of accounting
8.22 Loan capital
8.221 Debenture
8.222 Convertible loan stock
8.223 Redemption
8.23 Liabilities
8.231 Creditors *or* accounts payable
8.232 Secured creditors
8.233 Current liabilities
8.234 Contingent liabilities
8.235 Accrued expenses
8.24 Assets
8.241 Fixed assets
  8.241.1 Capital expenditure
  8.241.2 Book value
  8.241.3 Wasting assets
  8.241.4 Tangible assets
  8.241.5 Intangible assets
    8.241.51 Goodwill
    8.241.52 Fictitious assets
  8.241.6 Plant register
8.242 Investments
8.243 Sinking fund

Note: * Denotes a heading only – the term is not defined.

8.244 Current assets
8.244.1 Stocks
8.244.2 Raw materials
8.244.3 Bought out stocks
8.244.4 Work in progress
8.244.5 Finished goods
8.244.6 Debtors *or* accounts receivable
8.244.7 Payment in advance *or* prepayments
8.244.8 Liquid assets

8.245 Historical cost
8.246 Net assets
8.246.1 Net liquid funds

8.25 General terms

8.251 Capital commitment
8.252 Capital employed
8.253 Deferred expenditure
8.254 Deferred taxation
8.255 Pre-acquisition profits/losses
8.256 Provisions
8.257 Source and application of funds statement
8.258 Working capital

8.3 Revenue reporting*

8.31 Profit*
8.311 Gross profit
8.312 Net profit
8.313 Retained profits
8.314 Earnings per share
8.315 Dividend

8.32 Types of revenue accounts*
8.321 Trading account
8.322 Profit and loss account
8.323 Profit and loss appropriation account
8.324 Departmental accounts
8.325 Income and expenditure account
8.326 Receipts and payments account

Note: * Denotes a heading only – the term is not defined

8.33 General terms*
- 8.331 Extraordinary items
- 8.332 Prior year items
- 8.333 Revenue
- 8.334 Revenue expenditure
- 8.335 Sales turnover
- 8.336 Write off
  - 8.336.1 Preliminary expenses
  - 8.336.2 Amortization
  - 8.336.3 Bad debts
  - 8.336.4 Depreciation
  - 8.336.5 Obsolescence
  - 8.336.6 Redundancy

9. Nature and condition of organization*

9.1 Nature*
- 9.101 Prospectus
- 9.102 Company
  - 9.102.1 Chartered company
  - 9.102.2 Statutory company
  - 9.102.3 Registered company
    - 9.102.31 Company limited by shares (joint stock company)
    - 9.102.32 Private limited company
    - 9.102.33 Public limited company
    - 9.102.34 Company limited by guarantee
    - 9.102.35 Unlimited company
- 9.103 Subsidiary company
- 9.104 Holding Company
- 9.105 Group
- 9.106 Associated company
- 9.107 Partnership
- 9.108 Joint venture
- 9.109 Consortium
- 9.110 Acquisition or take-over
- 9.111 Merger

9.2 Condition*
- 9.21 Bankruptcy
  - 9.211 Statement of affairs
  - 9.212 Deficiency (or surplus) account
- 9.22 Insolvency
- 9.23 Overtrading
- 9.24 Over/under capitalized
- 9.25 Gearing

Note: * Denotes a heading only – the term is not defined

FINANCIAL ACCOUNTANCY

The profession whose members practise financial accounting, and the complex of principles, techniques and methods by means of which their expertise is put into effect.

6. FUNCTIONS

6.1 Financial accounting
The analysis, classification and recording of financial transactions, and the ascertainment of how such transactions affect the performance and financial position of an undertaking.

6.2 Book-keeping
The analysis, classification and recording of financial transactions in books of account.

6.3 Financial audit
A periodic examination of the books and records of a business carried out by a third party (the auditor), to ensure that they have been properly maintained.
Upon satisfactory completion of an audit a signed declaration is made to that effect.

7. BOOKS AND RECORDS

7.1 Basic concepts

7.101 Account
A record of transactions of a particular type, or with a particular person, usually expressed in financial terms and maintained in a ledger.

7.102 Posting
The recording of a transaction in a ledger account from a book of prime entry, or by transfer between ledger accounts.

7.103 Debit entry
A posting recording the *receipt* of value by an account. (e.g. the receipt of stock).

7.104 Credit entry
A posting recording the *giving* of value by an account (e.g. a payment to a supplier).

7.105 Contra
A book-keeping term meaning against, or on the opposite side. Usually used where debits are matched with related credits, in the same or a different account.

7.106 Double entry book-keeping
A system of book-keeping which reflects the dual aspect of each transaction by means of debit and credit entries in the books of account. The total of the debit entries should equal that of the credit entries at any time.

7.107 Single entry book-keeping
A system of book-keeping in which the dual aspect of transactions is ignored, and in which personal accounts only are maintained.

7.108 Balance (on an account)
The difference between the total debit and credit entries in an account.

7.109 Trial balance
A list of the debit and credit balances in the ledgers and the cash book, extracted at a given date. If the records have been correctly maintained under the double entry system the total of the debit balances will equal the total of the credit balances.

7.110 Books of account
The books of prime entry and the ledgers in which the financial transactions of a business are recorded.

7.111 Cut-off date
A date selected for isolating the flow of cash and goods, and the related documentation, to ensure that all aspects of a transaction are dealt with in the same financial period.

7.2 Books of prime entry

7.201 Day book
The record of all transactions of a particular category, prior to posting to the ledgers.

7.202 Journal
The terms journal and day book are synonymous when used to refer to a book of prime entry. In some cases the term journal has a narrow meaning and refers to the record of transactions, such as transfers between accounts and correction of book-keeping errors, which are not provided for in other books of prime entry.

7.203 Purchases day book
The record of details and amounts of each *credit* purchase.

7.204 Purchases returns book *or* returns outward book
The record of details and amounts of goods returned to suppliers.

7.205 Sales day book
The record of details and amounts of each *credit* sale.

7.206 Sales returns book *or* returns inwards book
The record of details and amounts of goods returned by customers.

7.207 Cash book
The record of cash receipts and payments.

7.207.1 Bank reconciliation
A detailed statement reconciling, at a given date, the cash balance reported by the bank with that shown in the records of a business.

7.208 Petty cash book
A separate record of small cash receipts and payments.

7.208.1 Imprest
A cash float, from which disbursements are made, which is periodically restored to its original amount.

7.3 Ledgers & Accounts

7.301 General, impersonal *or* nominal ledger
The record of accounts in which *all* transactions of a business are shown, in detail or in summary.

7.302 Purchases ledger *or* bought ledger
The record of creditors' individual accounts and transactions.

7.303 Sales ledger
The record of debtors' individual accounts and transactions.

7.304 Personal account
The record relating to a debtor or creditor.

7.305 Real *or* property account
The record of an asset (e.g. buildings, plant and equipment, cash, etc.).

7.306 Nominal account
A record of income and expenditure (e.g. sales, purchases).

7.307 Impersonal account
Any real or nominal account.

7.308 Suspense account
A ledger account in which items are held temporarily until sufficient information is available for them to be posted to the correct accounts.

7.309 Current account
The record of transactions between two businesses (usually members of the same group) or between head office and a branch, or between a bank and its customers.

7.310 Open account
An account showing a balance.

7.311 Control account
A total account inserted in a ledger (or section of accounts) to make it self-balancing. A run of debits and credits is posted to the individual ledger accounts, and the total is posted to the opposite side of the control account.

The term is sometimes applied only to the total accounts in the general ledger, in which case the total accounts in the other ledgers are called **adjustment accounts.**

8. FINANCIAL STATEMENT

Any form of statement setting out financial information. The term is most often used in connection with balance sheets or profit or loss.

8.1 Basic concepts

8.101 Fundamental accounting concepts

The broad basic assumptions which underlie the periodic financial accounts of business enterprises.

These concepts are set out and explained in *Statement of Standard Accounting Practice, No. 2*. (*SSAP No. 2*).

8.102 Accounting bases

The methods developed for applying fundamental accounting concepts to financial transactions and items, for the purpose of financial accounts, and in particular (a) for determining the account periods in which revenue and costs should be recognized in the profit and loss account, and (b) for determining the amounts at which material items should be stated in the balance sheet. (*SSAP No. 2*).

8.103 Accounting policies

The specific accounting bases selected and consistently followed by a business enterprise as being, in the opinion of the management, appropriate to its circumstances and best suited to present fairly its results and financial position. (*SSAP No. 2*).

8.104 Annual accounts

The set of accounts comprising the balance sheet as at a specified date, together with the profit and loss or other revenue account relating to the year which ended on the date of the balance sheet, and related notes which, in the case of companies, include the directors' report. Consolidated or group accounts are included if applicable. (The alternative term **final accounts** is sometimes applied).

8.105 Accounting period

The period of time covered by the financial statements of a business.

8.106 Group accounts

Financial statements of a group (*See* 9.105).

8.106.1 Consolidated financial statements

One form of group accounts which presents the information contained in the separate financial statements of a holding company and its subsidiaries as if they were the financial statements of a single entity.

8.107 Cash flow

A term used in connection with the cash generated during a given period.

For practical purposes, **cash flow forecasts** provide a means whereby managers can influence the balance between future cash income and cash expenditure.

8.2 Balance sheet

A statement of the financial position of an enterprise at a given date, normally based on historical cost and disclosing the book value of the assets, liabilities, share capital and reserves.

Note: The precise format of a balance sheet is not laid down by statute, but in the case of limited liability companies there are certain statutory requirements as to content.

8.21 Share capital and reserves

8.211 Share (in a joint stock company)

A fixed unit of capital contributed by a member of the company (i.e. a shareholder).

8.211.1 Ordinary shares

Shares which entitle the holders to the remaining divisible profits (and, in a liquidation, the assets) remaining after prior interests (e.g. preference shareholders) have been satisfied.

8.211.2 Preference shares

Shares carrying a fixed rate of dividend, the holders of which have a prior claim to any company profits available for distribution. These shareholders may also have a prior claim to the repayment of capital in the event of winding-up.

8.211.21 Cumulative preference shares

Shares which entitle the holders to a fixed rate of dividend, and the right to have any arrears of dividend paid out of future profits with priority over any distribution to the holders of equity share capital

8.211.22 Participating preference shares
Shares which usually entitle the holder to a fixed dividend, and to participate in any surplus profits after payment of dividends at a specified rate on the ordinary shares.

8.211.23 Redeemable preference shares
Shares which are repayable by a company, normally at a predetermined rate and time. Such repayment only applies to fully paid shares, and payment must be made out of profits or the proceeds of a new issue.

8.211.3 Deferred or **founders' shares**
A special class of shares in which the holders are not entitled to any dividend until the preference and ordinary share dividends have been paid. Some deferred shares carry no dividend entitlement until a specified future date.

These shares are usually of small nominal value as they carry a considerable proportion of the surplus profits after the dividend on the ordinary shares has reached a fixed rate. They are extremely valuable in a successful business.

8.211.4 Minority interests
Shares held in a subsidiary company by shareholders other than the holding company or its nominees.

8.211.5 Bonus or **scrip issue**
The capitalization of reserves by a company with the object of relating the issued share capital to the net assets employed.

This is done by issuing bonus shares to existing shareholders, in proportion to their holdings, such shares being normally fully paid-up. No monetary payments are made.

8.211.6 Rights issue
The raising of new capital by a company, by giving existing shareholders the right to subscribe to new shares or debentures in proportion to their current holdings.

A shareholder not wishing to take up a rights issue may sell the rights on the open market.

8.211.7 Non-voting shares
A class of shares which carry no voting rights.

8.211.8 Nominee holding
A shareholding in a company registered in the name of a nominee, instead of that of the owner.

8.212 Share capital

8.212.1 Authorized, nominal or **registered**
The number and amount of the shares which a company may issue, as empowered by its Memorandum of Association.

8.212.2 Issued or subscribed
The number and amount of the shares in circulation.

8.212.3 Unissued
The amount of the authorized share capital not in circulation.

8.212.4 Called-up
The amount which the company has required shareholders to pay on the shares issued.

8.212.5 Uncalled
The amount which the company has not required shareholders to pay on the shares issued.

8.212.6 Paid-up
The amount which shareholders are deemed to have paid on the shares issued and called-up.

8.212.7 Equity share capital
Issued share capital of a company which carries an unrestricted right to participate beyond a specified amount in a distribution.

8.212.8 Prior charge capital
Those classes of share and loan capital, the holders of which have a claim on the profit and assets of a business before the ordinary shareholders.

8.213 Reserves

Undistributed or surplus profits. The creation and distribution of certain reserves are affected by company policy and legal considerations, e.g. the provision of the Memorandum and Articles of Association of the company.

8.213.1 Capital reserves

Reserves which are not available for distribution as dividends, e.g. any surplus arising as a premium on the issue of shares or debentures. C.f. **revenue reserves.**

8.213.2 Revenue reserves

Reserves which are available for distribution as dividends. C.f. **capital reserves.**

8.214 Share premium

An excess paid to a company by a member, either in cash or other consideration, over the nominal value of the shares issued.

8.214.1 Share premium account

The account to which a share premium must be credited.

8.215 Equity

The equity share capital, plus reserves.

8.216 Net worth

A concept denoting the excess of the book values of all assets over liabilities. In a company it represents the interests of the shareholders, i.e. the paid-up share capital and any reserves. If the assets are taken at current values, instead of book values, the concept is known as **current worth.**

8.217 Equity method of accounting

A method of accounting under which the investment in a company is shown in the consolidated balance sheet at:

(a) the cost of the investment;

and

(b) the investing company or group's share of the post-acquisition retained profits and reserves of the company; less

(c) any amounts written off in respect of (a) and (b) above;

and under which the investing company accounts separately in its profit and loss account for its share of the profits before tax, taxation and extraordinary items of the company concerned. (*Definition from SSAP 14*).

8.22 Loan capital

Debentures and other fixed loans of a business. The holders of loan capital are normally paid a fixed rate of interest but do not share in the profits of a business.

8.221 Debenture

The written acknowledgement of a debt by a company, usually given under its Seal, and normally containing provisions as to payment of interest and repayment of principal. A debenture is frequently secured on some or all of the assets of the company.

8.222 Convertible loan stock

A loan which gives the holder the right to convert to other securities, normally ordinary shares, at a predetermined rate and time.

8.223 Redemption

Repayment. This term is most frequently used in connection with preference shares and debentures.

8.23 Liabilities

The financial obligations of a business, internal (e.g. to shareholders) and external (e.g. to creditors, debenture holders and in the case of a bank loan, the bank).

8.231 Creditors or **accounts payable**

Suppliers and others to whom money is owed. (See also 8.235 **Accrued expenses.**)

8.232 Secured creditors

Creditors whose claims are wholly or partly secured on the assets of a business.

8.233 Current liabilities

Liabilities which fall due for payment in a relatively short period, normally less than twelve months, e.g. creditors, bank overdrafts and provision for taxation and dividend claims.

8.234 Contingent liabilities

Obligations which may arise in respect of past or future events (e.g. the outcome of a patent infringement).

8.235 Accrued expenses

Expenses which are recognized when goods received or services provided during a given accounting period have not been invoiced, or when wages have been earned but not paid, by the end of that period.

8.24 Assets

Anything of value, owned by a business.

8.241 Fixed assets

Assets acquired for retention in a business for the purpose of providing goods or services. Fixed assets are not held for resale in the normal course of business.

8.241.1 Capital expenditure

The original or additional expenditure on fixed assets. Such expenditure relates to benefits in *future* periods. C.f. **revenue expenditure.** (8.334).

8.241.2 Book value

Book value refers to the historical cost of an asset, less the depreciation accumulated over its life to date, as opposed to its current market value.

8.241.3 Wasting assets

Assets of a fixed nature which are gradually consumed or exhausted in the process of earning income (e.g. mines or quarries).

8.241.4 Tangible assets

Assets having a physical identity (e.g. plant and machines).

8.241.5 Intangible assets

Assets which do not have a physical identity (e.g. goodwill).

8.241.51 Goodwill

The intangible benefit arising from the commercial connections and reputation of a business.

When a business is purchased, any amount paid in excess of its net worth represents the value placed on the goodwill.

8.241.52 Fictitious assets

Items shown as assets in a balance sheet which have no realizable value (e.g. the preliminary and formation expenses of a company, or special advertizing).

8.241.6 Plant register

A record showing details of each item of plant purchased and used by a business.

8.242 Investments

Any application of money, or money's worth, which is intended to return interest, income, profit or other benefit.

8.243 Sinking fund

A fund created for the redemption of a liability, or with the object of replacing an asset, by setting aside a sum periodically, and investing it (usually outside the business) so as to produce the required amount at the appropriate time.

8.244 Current assets

Cash or other assets (e.g. stocks or short term investments) held for conversion into cash in the normal course of trading.

8.244.1 Stocks

Raw materials, work in progress, finished goods and goods in transit, or on consignment, at the end of an accounting period.

8.244.2 Raw materials

Unprocessed stocks awaiting conversion into saleable products.

8.244.3 Bought out stocks

Stocks bought outside the business for eventual incorporation in finished goods, or for resale.

8.244.4 Work in progress

Materials, components or products in various stages of completion during a manufacturing process. The term also applies to partly completed contracts.

8.244.5 Finished goods
Manufactured goods, ready for sale or dispatch to a customer, agent, etc.

8.244.6 Debtors or **accounts receivable**
Customers, or others, owing money to the business.

8.244.7 Payments in advance or **prepayments**
Expenditure on goods or services for future benefit, which is to be charged to the cost of future operations. These amounts are usually included in **debtors** at the end of the period in which they are incurred.

8.244.8 Liquid assets
Cash, and other assets readily convertible into cash.

8.245 Historical cost
The original cost of acquiring assets, or of purchasing goods and services.

8.246 Net assets
The excess of the book value of the assets of a business over its liabilities (including loan capital).

8.246.1 Net liquid funds
Cash at bank and in hand and cash equivalents (e.g. investments held as current assets) less bank overdrafts and other borrowings repayable within one year of the accounting date. (*Definition from SSAP 10*).

8.25 General terms

8.251 Capital commitment
Future capital expenditure in respect of which contracts have been made.

8.252 Capital employed
The long term finances used by a business. In the case of a limited company the capital employed comprises the share and loan capital, with any retained profit and other reserves.

8.253 Deferred expenditure
Expenditure incurred during an accounting period, but not fully charged against income in that period, the balance

being carried forward and charged in the next or a subsequent period.

8.254 Deferred taxation
Taxation attributable to differences between profits as computed for taxation purposes and profits as stated in financial accounts which result from the inclusion of items of income and expenditure in taxation computations in periods different from those in which they are included in financial accounts. Timing differences originate in one period and are capable of reversal in one or more subsequent periods. In addition the revaluation of an asset is regarded as creating a timing difference when it is incorporated in accounts. (*Definition from SSAP 11*).

8.255 Pre-acquisition profits/losses
The profits or losses of a subsidiary company, attributable to a period prior to its acquisition by a holding company.

8.256 Provisions
Amounts written off or retained, by way of providing for depreciation, renewals or diminution of assets, or retained to provide for a known liability, the extent of which cannot be expressly determined.

8.257 Source and application of funds statement
A financial statement which shows the external and internal sources from which funds have been obtained to finance a business during a given accounting period, and the manner in which the funds have been deployed.

8.258 Working capital
The capital available for conducting the day-to-day operations of an organisation; normally, the excess of current assets over current liabilities.

8.3 Revenue reporting

8.31 Profit

8.311 Gross profit
The profit on goods and services sold, i.e. the excess of the realized proceeds over their cost, before taking into account

expenses incurred in selling and distribution, and in administering the business.

8.312 Net profit

The gross profit, *less* expenses incurred in selling, distribution and in administering the business.
Net profits can be shown *before* or *after taxation.*

8.313 Retained profits

Profits retained in the business, and not distributed to the owners/shareholders.

8.314 Earnings per share

The profit, in pence, attributable to each equity share, based on the consolidated profit of the period, after tax and after deducting minority interests and preference dividends, but before taking into account extraordinary items, divided by the number of equity shares in issue and ranking for dividend in respect of the period.
(*Definition from SSAP 3*).

8.315 Dividend

A distribution to shareholders out of profits, usually in the form of cash.

8.32 Types of revenue accounts

8.321 Trading account

A financial statement which shows the revenue from sales, the cost of those sales and the gross profit arising during a given accounting period.

8.322 Profit and loss account

A financial statement which shows the net profit or loss of a business for a given accounting period.

A detailed profit and loss account will normally show the gross profit (from the trading account) and the various expenses incurred in selling goods or services, and in administering and financing the business.

8.323 Profit and loss appropriation account

A financial statement which shows how the net profit, after

taxation, of the business has been distributed over dividends, transfers to reserves, profit retentions, etc.

8.324 Departmental accounts
Financial statements which show the profits or losses of the various departments of a business for a given accounting period. They normally take the form of a trading and a profit and loss account for each department.

8.325 Income and expenditure account
A financial statement often used by non-profit-making concerns such as clubs, associations, charities, etc., to show the excess of income over expenditure (or vice versa) for a given accounting period. The statement is similar to a profit and loss account.

8.326 Receipts and payments account
A financial statement which shows in summarized form the cash transactions during a given accounting period. It includes the opening and closing balances of cash in hand and/or at the bank.

8.33 General terms

8.331 Extraordinary items
Those items which derive from events or transactions outside the ordinary activities of the business and which are both material and expected not to recur frequently or regularly. They do not include items which, though exceptional on account of size and incidence (and which may therefore require separate disclosure), derive from the ordinary activities of the business. Neither do they include prior year items merely because they relate to a prior year.
(*Definition from SSAP 6* (*Revised*)).

8.332 Prior year items
Material adjustments applicable to prior years arising from changes in accounting policies and from the correction of fundamental errors. They do not include the normal recurring corrections and adjustments of accounting estimates made in prior years.
(*Definition from SSAP 6* (*Revised*)).

8.333 Revenue

This term is usually taken to mean the *income* of a business, i.e. the proceeds of sales, investment income, etc.

8.334 Revenue expenditure

Expenditure to maintain asset value (e.g. repairs) or to obtain revenue (e.g. raw materials, wages). C.f. **capital expenditure** (8.241.1).

8.335 Sales turnover

The net sales of a business, i.e. gross sales *less* discounts and sales returns.

8.336 Write off

To charge all or part of the book value of an asset against profits (e.g. obsolete stocks, bad debts, etc.).

8.336.1 Preliminary expenses

Expenses relating to the formation of a company. They include the cost of the company Memorandum and Articles of Association, the company Seal and Prospectus, and of related documentation.

Such expenses are normally written off as soon as possible.

8.336.2 Amortization

The provision for the extinction of a liability, or for the replacement of an asset, normally by means of a **sinking fund.**

The term is also used in connection with writing off the cost of a lease over the period of its life.

8.336.3 Bad debts

Those debts owed to a business which are regarded as uncollectable, and which may be written off.

8.336.4 Depreciation

The measure of the wearing out, consumption or other loss of value of a fixed asset whether arising from use, effluxion of time or obsolence through technology and market changes.

(*Definition from SSAP 12*).

8.336.5 Obsolescence

The measure of the loss of value of a fixed asset due to (a) its supersession by one which is technologically superior or (b) a cessation of the need for its use in consequence of a change in the marketing/production programme.

9. NATURE OR CONDITION OF ORGANIZATION

9.1 Nature

9.101 Prospectus

An invitation to the public to apply for the shares or debentures of a company.

9.102 Company

A company is a legal entity, the life of which is independent of that of its members.

There are three main ways of forming companies, namely, by charter, by legislation or by registration under the Companies Acts.

9.102.1 Chartered Company

A Chartered Company is formed by the grant of a Charter by the Crown. The Charter authorizes the company to operate and states the powers specifically granted. These days, Charters are normally only granted to associations having non-profit-making objectives.

9.102.2 Statutory Company

A Statutory Company is formed by Act of Parliament. The Act defines the powers of the company and authorizes its operations. These days, this method of company formation is normally confined to bodies of a governmental or semi-governmental nature such as the nationalized industries.

9.102.3 Registered Company

Most commercial companies are formed by registration under the Companies Act in force at the time. A Registered Company is legally constituted by means of its Memorandum of Association, which defines its objects and powers, and by its Articles of Association, which define the rules and regulations governing the management of its affairs, the rights of the members of the company, and the duties and powers of the directors.

9.102.31 Company limited by shares (or **joint stock company)**
A company in which the liability of members for the company's debts is limited to the amount, if any, unpaid on the shares taken up by them.

9.102.32 Private limited company
A private limited company is one whose Articles of Association:
(a) restrict the right to transfer its shares,
(b) limit the number of members to fifty, and
(c) prohibit any invitation to the public to subscribe to any shares or debentures in the company.

9.102.33 Public limited company
Any limited company which is not a private limited company, as defined at 9.102.32 above.

9.102.34 Company limited by guarantee
A company in which each member undertakes, on a winding-up, to contribute (to the limit of his guarantee) towards the payment of the liabilities of the company.

9.102.35 Unlimited company
A company in which the liability of the members is unlimited, i.e. every shareholder of the company is liable for the debts of the company.

9.103 Subsidiary company
A company shall be deemed to be a subsidiary of another if but only if,
(a) that other either:
 (i) is a member of it and controls the composition of its Board of Directors; or
 (ii) holds more than half in nominal value of its equity share capital; or
(b) the first mentioned company is a subsidiary of any company which is that other's subsidiary.
and it otherwise comes within the terms of Section 154 of the Companies Act 1948. (*Definition from SSAP 14*).

9.104 Holding company

A company is a holding company of another if but only if that other is its subsidiary as defined above.

9.105 Group

A holding company and its subsidiaries.

9.106 Associated company

A company (not being a subsidiary of the investing group or company) is an associated company of the investing group or company if:

(a) the investing group or company's interest in the associated company is effectively that of a partner in a joint venture or consortium, *or*

(b) the investing group or company's interest in the associated company is for the long term, and is substantial (i.e. not less than 20% of the equity voting rights), and, having regard to the disposition of the other shareholdings, the investing group or company is in a position to exercise a significant influence over the associated company.

In both cases it is essential that the investing group or company participates (usually through representation on the board) in commercial and financial policy decisions of the associated company, including the distribution of profits. (*Definition from SSAP 1*).

9.107 Partnership

A relationship between persons carrying on a business in common with a view to profit.

The liability of the individual partners is unlimited, unless the partnership agreement provides for any limitation. A partnership consists of not more than twenty persons, except in certain cases, e.g. practising solicitors, professional accountants and members of the Stock Exchange, where this figure may be exceeded.

9.108 Joint venture

The agreement of two persons or organizations to join together, normally in connection with a single operation, in which their individual business capabilities and trading interests may be profitably combined.

9.109 Consortium

An association of several businesses with a view to carrying out a joint activity.

A separate organization may, or may not, be created for the management of the activity.

9.110 Acquisition or **take-over**

The acquiring, by one business, of a controlling interest in another. (*See also*, **holding company** 9.104 *and* **subsidiary company** 9.103).

9.111 Merger

The amalgamation of two or more separate businesses. A merger is normally brought about by an exchange of shares.

9.2 Condition

9.21 Bankruptcy

An act or default by a debtor which is deemed to be evidence of his insolvency.

9.211 Statement of affairs

A statement, in a prescribed form, showing the estimated financial position of a debtor. It contains a summary of the debtor's total assets and liabilities. The assets are shown at their estimated realizable values. The various classes of creditors, such as preferential, secured, partly secured and unsecured, are shown separately.

9.212 Deficiency (or **surplus) account**

A statement, in a prescribed form, which shows the excess, if any, of liabilities over assets, or vice versa, at a given date. The account shows how the debtor has arrived at his present position.

The balance on this account, either a surplus or a deficiency, must agree with that shown on the Statement of Affairs.

9.22 Insolvency

A business is said to be insolvent if it is unable to meet its financial obligations.

9.23 Overtrading

A term applied to a business which enters into commitments in excess of its available resources, i.e. is undercapitalized. (See over/under capitalized, 9.24.)

9.24 Over/under capitalized

Terms used to describe a surplus or deficiency of capital in relation to the current level of activity of a business.

9.25 Gearing

The relationship between prior charge capital (i.e. debt and preference capital) on the one hand and equity share capital and reserves on the other. Debt includes fixed interest loans and net short-term borrowings.

The company having a high proportion of prior charge capital to equity is 'high-geared', and is 'low-geared' if the reverse situation applies.

INDEX

Figures in bold type indicate diagrams.

ICMA publications

Analysing Business Strategy: Cost—volume—profit analysis
Analysing Uncertainty: quantitative forecasting
An Introduction to Business Forecasting
Business Mathematics
Classification and Coding of Accounts
Corporate Planning
Cost of Labour Turnover
Cost and Management Accountancy for Students (ICMA/Heinemann)
Cost Reduction
Current Cost Accounting and Management Decisions
Disclosure of Financial Information to Employees
Engineer's Guide to Costing (revised 1978)
Investment Appraisal, Evaluating Risk and Uncertainty

Management Accounting in Inflation Series
Management Accounting in Inflationary Conditions
Corporate Planning in inflationary conditions
Forecasting Costs & Prices: Theory & Practice
Forecasting Exchange Rates: Theory & Practice
Pricing

Management Information Systems and the Computer Series
Part I —The Design of the Management Information Systems
Part II —Computer Applications, Section 1
Part II —Computer Applications, Section 2
Part III—Cost Effectiveness from Computer Expenditure
Part IV—Cost Control of Data Processing Activities
Mathematical Tables for Students
Profitable Use of Capital in Industry
Report Writing in Business
The Structure of Consolidated Accounting: H. K. Jaeger (ICMA/Macmillan)
Terminology of Management and Financial Accountancy
Value Added: B. Cox (ICMA/Heinemann)
Variance Accounting: E. Laidler (ICMA/Macmillan)

All the above may be obtained from Publications Manager, Institute of Cost and Management Accountants, 63 Portland Place, London W1N 4AB.

Blackfords of Truro and London